Victorious Affirmations For Women

Winning Affirmations for Women

Written By:
Tiffany Easley

A Suber Media Group Project
©2010 by Tiffany Easley

All rights reserved. No portion of this book may be reproduced, stored in a retrieval system, or transmitted in any form or by any means-electronic, mechanical, photocopy, recording, scanning or other - except for brief quotations in reviews or articles without the prior written consent of the publisher

ISBN: 978-0-9841815-8-2

FORWARD

As you journey through life, you will face many situations. Some will be easier than others. Some may cause you to rejoice, others may cause you to cry and some may even cause you to laugh. It is in each situation along life's journey that you are being fashioned by God from the inside out. You may encounter many situations which make you feel as though you are battling for your life. Battiling without the power and strength you need to fight. Suddenly you have begun to think as a victim and not a Victor.

There may be days when you may feel as though you cannot go on. You may feel that you have no fight left for the battle. These are the days that you can pick up Victorious Affirmations for Women and be affirmed as the Champion that God called you to be. You will be reminded that you are victorious in all things Remember that it is the Lord your God who goes with you to fight for you against your enemies to give you victory. Deuteronomy 20:1-4. Each affirmation intends to pull from your inner strength. The reflective exercises will help you identify areas for personal development ensuring that you will reign in victory. Get your journal and begin to journal your questions and answers to the reflective exercises.

You will be encouraged to believe in who God says you are. You will be empowered to walk the journey in confidence knowing you have victory over every situation you face. You will be enlightened on the importance of believing, speaking, and walking in victory. Your time to be victorious begins now and from this day forward you are affirmed as a Victorious Woman!

Tiffany Easley

Author

Contents

Affirmation: I am Beautiful — 10

Affirmation: I am Bold — 13

Affirmation: I am Boundless — 15

Affirmation: I am Chosen — 17

Affirmation: I am Called — 19

Affirmation: I am Consecrated — 21

Affirmation: I am a Prayer Warrior — 23

Affirmation: I am a Peace Maker — 25

Affirmation: I am a Woman of Praise and Worship — 27

Affirmation: I am Energized to Energize others — 29

Affirmation: I am Empowered to Empower others — 31

Affirmation: I am a Visionary — 34

Affirmation: I am Anointed — 38

Affirmation: I am Appointed — 40

Affirmation: I am Assigned — 42

Affirmation: I am Focused	*44*
Affirmation: I am Fashioned	*46*
Affirmation: I am Faithful	*48*
Affirmation: I am Dedicated	*50*
Affirmation: I am Determined	*52*
Affirmation: I am Destined	*54*
Affirmation: I am Fearfully and Wonderfully made	*56*
Affirmation: I am Victorious	*58*
Affirmation: I am Celebrated	*60*

Affirmation: *I* am Beautiful

Life is full of clichés that surround the word "beauty" and its meaning. The most common two are "beauty is in the eye of the beholder" and "beauty is only skin deep". The world has its own way of defining beauty which has created images that are not rootend in Kingdom principles. They have caused a decrease of low self-esteem, self-image, and self-worth. As we begin to meditate on this first Affirmation: "I am beautiful", I want you to really think on the things of God when determining your self-esteem, self-image and self-worth. As Ecclesiastes 3:11 tells us. God has made everything beautiful in its time! My sister my friend.. You are beautiful. Let's take this a little deeper. When you look in the mirror you see a reflection of yourself. In that reflection, you are able to see all that is good and bad with your exterior image. Through this short affirmation I encourage you to take a different perspective on what you are seeing. While that mirror may point out flaws in your skin (i.e. pimples, blemishes, and our physical scars) it does not allow you to see your "perfect beauty". See the beauty that radiates from within that is made by your heavenly creator. The word "beautiful" is defined in many ways, but as we began this journey in victorious affirmations I believe we need to look at the following definition. "Beauty" is defined as "excellent" which simply means "very good of its kind: eminently good".

The fullness of your beauty may not yet be revealed but as the word of God says, He has made everything beautiful in its time. You are more than your physical attributes you are more than what looks good to the natural eye you are excellent my sister. You are beautiful!

Prayer: Lord thank You for affirming my beauty. Thank You for allowing me to see my beauty through Your eyes, for everything that You made is beautiful. God as I began to reflect over this affirmation and complete the reflective exercises, allow the Holy Spirit to remove any hindrances or distractions from my thoughts. Help me to see Kingdom Beauty and to recognize the beauty within me. In Jesus Name, Amen.

Reflective Exercise

1-Make a list of 5 qualities you have (do not include any physical qualities).

2-How do the 5 qualities you listed in question one make you spiritually beautiful?

3-After affirming your beauty what steps are you going to take to ensure that your beauty shines in the Kingdom?

4-Look into a mirror and describe yourself based on what you cannot see. This is your true Kingdom beauty.

Affirmation: *I am Bold*

Are you bold for the Kingdom? To be "bold" means to be fearless before danger; showing or requiring a fearless daring spirit. Do you dare to be different? Do you dare to take a stand for what is right no matter what it may cost you? In the book of Esther, we become acquainted with a Jewish girl who took a stand for her people. In the same way that Esther decided to make a stand and free her people: you have to decide to make a stand in the Kingdom and be bold and different. Do not worry because you do not look like others. Do not worry because you do not walk and talk like others. Instead, focus on the confidence that God has given to you. The bible says in 2 Timothy 1:7 "For God did not give us a spirit of timidity (of cowardice, of craven and cringing and fawning fear), but [He has given us a spirit] of power and of love and of calm and well-balanced mind and discipline and self-control". So starting today you will walk in boldness, You will claim territory for the Kingdom of God and you will no longer live in fear. You will no longer be afraid of what others think about you. You will no longer be afraid to step out on faith and do what God has called you to do. You will reign over fear and you will leap bountifully into new territory; where you will take the enemy by force, freeing family, friends, and co-laborers. You will be bold for the Kingdom.

Victorious Affirmations For Women

Prayer: Lord thank You for the spirit of boldness. I am grateful that I do not have to live in fear. God, as I begin to reflect over this affirmation and complete the reflective exercises, allow the Holy Spirit to remove any hindrances or distractions from my thoughts. Help me to expose any areas where I may still be dealing with fear and once those areas have been exposed, Lord, help me to allow the Holy Spirit to come in those areas and purge those things not like You. Help me to be dedicated in becoming a bold vessel for Your Kingdom! In Jesus Name, Amen.

Reflective Exercise

1- What is your greatest fear?

2- List (5) action steps you will take to overcome your greatest fear?

3- Find someone who you can partner with as an accountability partner and can help you with your commitment to complete the 5 action steps you listed in question 2.

Affirmation: *I* am Boundless

If there were no limits to what you could attain in life, would you not reach for it all? In the kingdom of God, you have it all; you are boundless in God. Your territory extends North, South, East, and West. You have no boundaries in God. You are boundless. Walk in the authority that He has given you; and do as God has instructed you to do. God's word says in Deuteronomy 11:24 "every place on which the sole of your foot treads shall be yours: from the wilderness and Lebanon, from the river, the River Euphrates, even to the Western Sea, shall be your territory". Are you bound to some things in life? If so, it is time to lose them. God has given you freedom in all things and the ability to live freely. If you are bound to an unhealthy relationship now is the time to break those ties. If you are tied to a dead end job, now is the time to step out on faith and shake the dust proclaiming victory for a new job. Stop letting the things of this world keep you bound. Take the chains off; the sky is the limit. You are not bound, but are boundless in Christ!

Prayer: Dear Lord Jesus, thank You for the ability to live a life in liberty and freedom. Help me to recognize that there are no chains holding me. God as I begin to reflect over this affirmation and complete the reflective exercises, allow the Holy Spirit to remove any hindrances or distractions from my thoughts. Guide me in this reflective exercise and expose the areas that are not like You. In Jesus Name, Amen.

Reflective Exercise

1- Identify (3) areas in your life that you feel you are bound and have no freedom.

2- Choose (1) of the areas from question 1 and list (3) action steps to begin walking in freedom within this area.

3- Once you have began to walk in freedom in this (1) area write what you will do to help others obtain their freedom?

Affirmation: *I* am Chosen

It is no mistake that you are living in purpose. God chose you. Not only did he choose you, he chose you with a specific purpose in mind. God's word tells us that we have been chosen to bear fruit. This fruit will last, so that whatever you ask in your Father's name He will do it. When you are "chosen" it means that you are one who is the object of choice or divine favor; an elect person. You are elected by Christ to be part of His family to bear fruit (produce). God wants you to produce results for the Kingdom. You have been chosen to share your testimony, to share your Christian experience, to share your journey from before Christ to now. You have been chosen to be a light in a dark place. You have been chosen to share your light with the dark world. Be the light to the drug addicted, to the oppressed, and to those who are lost. Since you have been chosen, are you living up to your potential? Are you operating in your "chosen" purpose? God has plans for you; and they are to prosper you, to give you hope and a future. Are you living out that chosen purpose? It is time to get busy, chosen woman of God! You have to choose to operate as the chosen Kingdom woman that God created you to be.

Prayer: Lord God, thank You for choosing me. Help me to reflect on Your affirmation of being chosen and to identify the importance of being chosen. God, as I begin to reflect over this affirmation and complete the reflective exercises, allow the Holy Spirit to remove any hindrances or distractions from my thoughts. Open my mind and my heart so I may walk as a chosen woman of God. In Jesus Name, Amen.

Reflective Exercise

1- In being chosen; what are you willing to do so that the world can see the light of Jesus operate through you?

2- Being "chosen" means that you are the object of God's favor. You have the ability to receive great things because you are a child of the King. In receiving favor how will you favor others?

3- How will you choose to represent the Kingdom as God's chosen vessel?

Affirmation: *I* am Called

When a telephone rings you immediately know two things: (1) someone wants to talk and (2) a voice will be heard on the other end. The world is so advanced now, that you do not have to be at home to receive a call. In fact you can receive a call anywhere because cellular phones allow us to be mobile. Just as you receive "calls" in your natural life by way of telephone, mobile or land line; there is a call that you have to receive in your spiritual life. What is God calling you to do in His Kingdom? Are you positioning yourself to hear the call of the Lord? In order to hear that call, you may have to be in a place of solitude. In order to decipher that call you may have to let go of family or friends. You may have to change geographical location. Just as in answering the telephone when it rings, you have to answer God when He calls. No matter what He is calling you to, you have a responsibility to answer. So listen closely, pay attention to "all" things. God may call you to a particular person, group of people, a specific geo- graphic location, a particular cause; whatever it may be, you have a responsibility to answer the call. Get up and answer the call of God, you never know where it will lead.

Prayer: Dear Lord Jesus thank You for Your call to the King- dom. God as I begin to reflect over this affirmation and complete the reflective exercises, allow the Holy Spirit to remove any hin- drances or distractions from my thoughts. Help me to recognize my calling and to operate in that calling within every area of my life. Help me to reflect openly and honestly in the following reflective exercises so that spiritual growth can occur. In Jesus Name, Amen.

Reflective Exercise

1- What have you been called to do in the Kingdom?

2- Share what your "calling" experience was like.

3- Have you completely answered the call? If so, how are you operating in the call? If not, what will you do to begin operating in your call to the Kingdom?

Affirmation: *I* am Consecrated

To all my single ladies, this affirmation is for you! Listen to me and listen to me good. As you read the words, "I am consecrated" I want you to understand that this is majorly important in the Kingdom of God. To be "consecrated" means to "make or declare sacred or to devote to a purpose with or as if with deep solemnity or dedication". The word of God tells us in Jeremiah 1:5, "Before I formed you in the womb I knew [and] approved of you [as My chosen instrument], and before you were born I separated and set you apart, consecrating you; [and] I appointed you as a prophet to the nations". Ladies hear me... God has set you apart for a reason. You are top quality, you are special and unique, there is none like you. You deserve to be treated with great respect from all people. God set you apart with a unique design and in doing so; He consecrated you for the Kingdom. Never let anyone treat you as though you are less of a person, that your purpose is not impor- tant, or that you cannot reach your goals. You are Consecrated, you have been purposed for the Kingdom for such a time as this. In fact you have been declared as sacred (devoted exclusively to one service or use)! Do not devote yourself for a use that is not rooted in Kingdom principles.

Prayer: Thank you God for consecrating me and setting me apart. God, as I begin to reflect over this affirmation and complete the reflective exercises, allow the Holy Spirit to remove any hindrances or distractions from my thoughts. Help me to identify a plan for successfully living a consecrated lifestyle. Help me to look deep within to determine hindrances that are stopping my ability to live a consecrated lifestyle. In Jesus Name, Amen.

Reflective Exercise

1- Have you made a conscious decision to live a consecrated lifestyle? If so, what steps did you take to become devoted to the Kingdom? If not, what steps are you willing to take to begin devoting yourself to the Kingdom?

2- What things/people are you devoted to that do not promote Kingdom living?

3- How will you begin to transition from those things/people that do not promote Kingdom living and began devoting your time, talent, and resources to the Kingdom?

Affirmation: *I am a Prayer Warrior*

Prayer is the key to communicating with God! You are a prayer warrior and it is your responsibility to war. Be a warrior for the Kingdom through prayer. We are instructed with very specific guidelines on how we should pray. In Philippians 4:6-8, the bible tells us "to be anxious for nothing, but in everything by prayer and supplication, with thanksgiving, let your requests be made known to God; and the peace of God, which surpasses all understanding, will guard your hearts and minds through Christ Jesus". In order to communicate with God you have to pray. Part of your responsibility to the Kingdom is to war on its behalf as a prayer warrior. Prayer is defined by Webster's dictionary as an address (as a petition) to God. It is important that you pray and consult God before moving forward with your daily endeavors. You must seek God and His instructions concerning all that you do, so that He can provide you with the wisdom and instruction. Teaching you how to be a blessing to the vision of the Kingdom. You must pray and war on behalf of the Kingdom so that you can intercede on the behalf of those who need the power of agreement! You must step up for the Kingdom today, Prayer Warrior; you must speak those things that are not as though they were. Pray without ceasing.

Prayer: Thank you God for giving me the ability to communicate with You through prayer. God as I began to reflect over this affirmation and complete the reflective exercises, allow the Holy Spirit to remove any hindrances or distractions from my thoughts. Thank you for hearing my every prayer and for honoring those request that line up with Your perfect Will. God teach me how to pray and what to pray for. Allow me to listen to You and to be obedient what You reveal through my time in prayer. Help me to war on the behalf of the Kingdom changing the atmosphere and setting the tone for Kingdom. In Jesus Name, Amen.

Reflective Exercise

1- What does your prayer time with God look like? How can you enhance this experience?

2- Do you keep a journal of your request and make note of what God has spoken to you during your prayer time? If not, will you commit to start? Are you willing to start journaling your experience?

3- Create an action plan detailing your prayer time with God. Include the days/times you will pray and journal with God. Find an accountability partner to help you stay on target with your action plan.

Affirmation: *I* am a Peace Maker

This world has been seeing many unsettling things happen. Their have been hurricanes (Louisiana), to earthquakes (Haiti), and now the severe flooding (Tennessee). In lieu of all of this, many would say that the world is far from peace. With war still raging in the Northeast, the world as we know it has to work at achiev- ing peace. The world may have to work at achieving peace, but the Kingdom of God should be at peace and remain at that place of peace in spite of what is going on around them. We are peace makers, meaning that we make peace no matter where we are. In the midst of an argument, we make peace, in the midst of a domestic disturbance, we make peace, in the midst of an unstable work envi- ronment, we make peace. The word of God tells us in Colossians 3:15 to let the peace of God rule in our hearts! You are equipped to make peace in ALL given situations. You are a peace maker; it is in your spiritual DNA!

Prayer: God I thank You that in all situations You have given me peace. God as I begin to reflect over this affirmation and complete the reflective exercises, allow the Holy Spirit to re- move any hindrances or distractions from my thoughts You have allowed me to look beyond what is going on around me and find peace within my spirit man. God please continue to show me how to seek peace and pursue it in all situations. Help me Lord to always be a peace maker. In Jesus Name. Amen.

Reflective Exercise

1- Think of a situation where there was all kinds of chaos around you. In that situation could you find peace, did you attempt to function as a peacemaker, if so please share that experience?

2- Where is it most difficult for you to find peace and why?

3- Share an experience where you took part in chaos instead of operating in peace. Having hindsight on that situation, list those things that you could have done differently and how you would encourage others to react in a peaceful manner?

Affirmation: *I* am a Woman of Praise and Worship

It is necessary that we praise God for what He does and we worship God for who He is! You must praise the Lord! He tells us in His word, let everything that has breath praise the Lord, praise ye the Lord. Are you praising God? Are you worshiping God? When life is good or bad and things happen, do you praise God? When God blesses you, when your prayers are manifested do you praise God? When you enter His sanctuary is your mind set on who He is or what He has done? Are you ready to be a woman of praise and worship? As a woman of praise and worship you seek God's Kingdom first. As a woman of praise and worship you know who you are (in Christ) and you know who you belong to. As a woman of praise and worship you praise God no matter how things are going and even when God's answer is not right now, you praise Him for the time in His waiting chambers. You worship God in spirit and in truth. You worship God from a state of pure praise. Get busy and get your praise and worship on.

Prayer: God I thank You for the ability to praise You with everything that I have. God as I began to reflect over this affirma- tion and complete the reflective exercises, allow the Holy Spirit to remove any hindrances or distractions from my thoughts. God I thank You for all that you have done, are doing, and will do in the future. I thank You for Your son Jesus who died for my sins and I thank You for the gift of eternal life. God help me to become a woman of praise and worship. Help me to have a mind and spirit that it grounded in them both. In Jesus Name. Amen.

Reflective Exercise

1- How do you get into the presence of God in worship?

2- Describe a moment when praising God was difficult for you. How did your overcome that difficulty?

3- In what environment do you find it most difficult to worship or praise God? How do you get past that difficulty?

Affirmation: *I* am Energized to Energize others

Are you vigorous and active? Do you impart energy to others? As a child of the most high God you are energized through the Holy Spirit to energize others. You are to impart wisdom, exhortation, and encouragement to the women of God. Your are to be a light to those who have not yet embraced the Kingdom of God to the fullest. The Holy Spirit gives you the ability to speak life over your circumstances. Through the personal experience of those circumstances, you are enabled to energize other people. You can speak to that sister who has experienced a valley in their life and through your transparency in sharing your valley experience. You can en- courage and empower others by speaking life to their experience. Through your spiritual energy and the experience of your journey you can energize others! The word of God says that in Him you live, move, and have your being. This statement gives you the au- thorization to energize others, because you have been energized by the Master himself. Get busy and go about the Kingdom full of energy and energizing others.

Prayer: God, thank You for the spiritual energy that You give to me and the ability to energize others. I am thankful for the journey of life You have assigned to me and the ability to use the experience of my journey to energize others. God help me to live each day to the fullest with your empowering grace and mercy. Help me to invigorate Your kingdom daughters. God, as I begin to reflect over this affirmation and complete the reflec- tive exercises, allow the Holy Spirit to remove any hindrances or distractions from my thoughts. In Jesus Name. Amen.

Reflective *Exercise*

1- What is your source of energy? Is it God? If it is not, what source are you relying on and why?

2- How do you use your personal journey to energize others?

3- Write an encouraging statement to your fellow sisters. Become transparent to them and allow your testimony to energize them!

Affirmation: *I am Empowered to Empower others*

Do you know who you are and who you belong to? Do you find yourself wanting to empower others? It is no surprise, because as a woman of God you are empowered to empower others. God wants to use all that you are and all that you go through as a testimony of the blessings that He has given you. God continually empowers His children through His mighty and living Word as well as through Kingdom network opportunities. What people, situations, or things empower you? Think of the last time that something extraordinary happened? Did you stop to think that the extraordinary happened in order to empower you so that you can empower someone else? Have you realized that it is in God that you live, move, and have your being? Because of this one fact you are empowered to empower others. The words you speak, the words you write, are a sounding board for you to encourage your fellow sisters. God has chosen you from the beginning of time. He has promised you that your boundary lines have fallen in pleasant places, that you are from above and not beneath. You are the apple of His eye. You have the God ordained mission to empower others because God continually empowers you.

Victorious Affirmations For Women

Through His Word (the Holy Bible) God empowers you, go em- power others! Through His prophets, teachers, evangelists, and preachers God empowers you; Go empower others! The word empower means to promote self actualization or influence. Who are you empowering to love with the love of God? Who are you speaking a word to and helping them see the goodness of God in them and others? Do you take time to help someone see better, see greater, see bigger by seeing the Jesus in them! Look within and draw from the power of your spirit woman/man. Then use that power to empower someone else.

Prayer: Dear Lord Jesus, we come before You with humble hearts. We rejoice in knowing that You are our reason for existence. It is you that created us in the likeness of Yourself. We thank You for the Holy Spirit that dwells within us. Thank You for giving us the ability and the power to share with others in a way that we can we can empower each others. We ask that from this experience You will show us who we should be surrounding ourselves with and to whom we should be speaking a word into, while allowing them to speak a word to us. God as I begin to reflect over this affirma- tion and complete the reflective exercises, allow the Holy Spirit to remove any hindrances or distractions from my thoughts Help us to become empowering vessels, working for the Glory of Your Kingdom. In Jesus Name. Amen.

Reflective Exercise

1- Describe yourself as an empowered individual. Paint a picture (using words) as to what your empowered self would look like.

2- What are some key elements you find necessary to reach a point of being empowered?

3- Share a situation where you felt powerless and share how you became powerful. How have you used that testimony to empower others?

Affirmation: *I am a Visionary*

A "visionary" is someone who has unusual foresight or imagination. God gave you the ability to see and envision. Are you using the gift? The Word tells us in Habakkuk 2:2, to write the vision and make it plain. Are you writing the vision? Every time you see (form a mental picture of) something or even someone, you are using the gift of vision. Now, the question is do you put the vision to work? You must work the vision for the Kingdom. The ideas (desires) that you have are not by happen stance; they have meaning and purpose. Put them to work. First, pray and ask God to develop/nurture the vision He has given to you. Next write it down (along with a plan of action). Then, walk out the vision for the Kingdom. We often times see a mental picture of where God wants to take us or wants to do in or through us, but we stop at the seeing of the vision. Today, I challenge you to go beyond seeing only and move into living out the vision. You have been given all that you need; you just have to start living the vision. God says you will be a mother, start living the vision. God says you will be a business owner, start living the vision. God says you will be an author, start living the vision. I have never known our God to tell you something and not show it to you. He does that so you can start putting the vision in action. Get busy and walk in your visionary anointing.

Victorious Affirmations For Women

Can you imagine having no vision? To not be able to see the sunshine, to see the birds flying, or see the smiles on your loved one's face. While many of us know individuals who have limited or no physical sight; have we ever stopped to think about what it is like to be a person with no spiritual vision? The lack of spiritual vision breeds lack of spiritual destination. If you cannot see where you are going, then you cannot get to a destination. Just as individuals who are visually impaired in the physical have the aide of seeing eye dogs, or magnifying glasses and braille documents, those who lack spiritual vision can obtain the visual assistance through prayer (communicating with God), through reading/studying the bible (discovering the path to the Kingdom), and worshipping God! It is important that as women we develop our Kingdom vision. We need to be able to see beyond the sur- face things and see into the Heavens. God desires that we oper- ate from a stance of spiritual 20/20 vision. God's Word in Habakkuk 2:2-3, tells us to write the vision and make it plain. How can we write a vision if we are not a visionary? Start looking, start seeing, start operating as a visionary. In Joel, chapter 2 the Word of God tells us, "And it shall come to pass afterward, that I will pour out my spirit upon all flesh; and your sons and your daughters shall prophesy, your old men shall dream dreams, your young men shall see visions: That time has come NOW!" Get busy fulfilling the visions that God has given you.

Victorious Affirmations For Women

Prayer: Dear Lord, I am grateful for my ability to see both physically and spiritually. God I thank You for every vision and dream that You give to me, knowing that they will bless your people and Your Kingdom. Help me to write the vision and make it plain so that those who read it can run with it. Help me Lord, to be a Kingdom Visionary and to operate as a seer while develop- ing the gift of vision. God, as I begin to reflect over this affirma- tion and complete the reflective exercises, allow the Holy Spirit to remove any hindrances or distractions from my thoughts. In Jesus Name, Amen.

Reflective Exercise

1- What is God showing you (His vision)?

2- What visions/dreams have you laid aside?

3- Use your response from question 2, to begin writing a personal vision statement. Think about the following: How do I see myself? What are my strengths and weaknesses and how do they work to develop the person that I have become?

Affirmation: *I am Annointed*

Have you ever wondered why some people are so good at what they do and they seem to do it with ease? Well I have an answer for you; it is because they are anointed. To be "anointed" means to be chosen by divine election. You have been chosen by the divine election of God for the Kingdom. You are an anointed vessel for God, to use in His Kingdom. He anoints your hands to use them for the Kingdom, He anoints your voice for you to use in His Kingdom. He anoints your eyes/ears for you to use in His Kingdom. God's word tells us in Luke 4:18, "The Spirit of the Lord is on me, because He has anointed me to preach good news to the poor." He has sent me to proclaim freedom for the prisoners and recovery of sight for the blind, to release the oppressed, to proclaim the year of the Lord's favor." You have been anointed with an anointing that is powerful beyond the enemies forces. Use your anointing to the glory of God's Kingdom.

Prayer: Thank you God for the anointing power! Thank you for allowing me to bless Your Kingdom and to flow under Your anointing power. Continue to help me mature the anointing that you have on my life and show me my areas of greatest anointing. If I am anointed as a visionary, help me to increase my vision. If I am anointed as a praise and worship leader, help me to in- crease my praise and worship Psalms of Praise. If I am anointed as a preacher/teacher, help me to increase my message. God, as I begin to reflect over this affirmation and complete the reflec- tive exercises, allow the Holy Spirit to remove any hindrances or distractions from my thoughts. In Jesus Name, Amen.

Reflective Exercise

1- Do you make it a practice to flow in the anointing? If not, why? And if so, how can you increase that flow?

2- Has a spiritual leader helped you to identify your area(s) of anointing? Do you seek to understand and develop those areas daily, why or why not?

3- Do you actively pray for God to open doors allowing you to use your anointing? When He opens those doors, do you feel comfortable flowing in the anointing? Please share the difficul- ties you may have experienced when flowing in your anointing, how did you learn to become comfortable in those times?

Affirmation: *I am Appointed*

You are appointed in the Kingdom of God. Your position is to rule over the earth. The key in this appointment is to walk in obedience to the Father. As early as Adam and Eve, God's divine plan appointed you over the earth! You are appointed to do great things by His anointing power and by application of God's Word. When someone is "appointed" they are fixed or officially set. You have been set in the Kingdom and your progress is fixed in eternity. You are officially a child of the most-high God (that is fixed: you are appointed). You are officially the head and not the tail (that is fixed; you are appointed). You are made in the image and likeness of God (that is fixed; you are appointed). Stop taking your appointment to the Kingdom lightly and start operating in your official set place. Begin to realize that where you are is not by mistake or by chance, but instead it is by divine purpose and intention. God has strategically set you where you are. You have been appointed to function in that set place.

Prayer: Thank You Lord for appointing me to this set place in my life. Thank You for developing and nurturing me so that I can walk uprightly in this appointed place in my life. I pray that You will guide my every decision and guard my every thought as I shoulder this divine appointment in life. God, as I begin to re- flect over this affirmation and complete the reflective exercises, allow the Holy Spirit to remove any hindrances or distractions from my thoughts. In Jesus Name, Amen.

Reflective *Exercise*

1- What is your level of understanding concerning your appointment in the Kingdom? How do you carry out this appointment?

2- In your current appointed place; what do you find to be the most difficult task; how are you dealing with that task?

3- What are a few encouraging words you can share with your fellow sisters concerning the difficulties they are facing in their appointed (set) place?

Affirmation: *I am Assigned*

Think back to a time when you were in school or taking a class and the teacher would give you assignments. Would you agree that some of those assignments were exciting, some were not so exciting, a few were hard and some may have been easy? Did you find yourself not wanting to finish an assignment or even not completely understanding what the teacher wanted you to gain out of the assignment? Believe it or not, you have assignments in the Kingdom of God that you are expected to complete. God's plan for your life has a blue print and within that blue print He has given you a number of assignments. Some assignments can be completed alone; others may have to be completed in a group setting. You even have certain individuals that are assigned to you. There are individuals in certain seasons of your life that God will assign to help you in certain situations and then you may be assigned to help others. God has a plan for your life and it is rooted in promotion, but you have to complete some assignments in order to obtain promotion and eventually graduate. Embrace your Kingdom assignments, promotion is in the air, but you must do your homework first.

Prayer: God I thank You for the assignments You have placed in my life. I pray for strength to endure those assignments which are not pleasant, wisdom for those assignments that are most challenging, and for guidance with those assignments that I may not understand. Thank You God for the homework that will aide in Kingdom promotion and graduation into eternal life. God as I began to reflect over this affirmation and complete the reflec- tive exercises, allow the Holy Spirit to remove any hindrances or distractions from my thoughts In Jesus Name, Amen.

Reflective Exercise

1- In recognizing your Kingdom assignments, what has been one of your most difficult to complete?

2- When faced with a difficult assignment in the Kingdom, how did you maintain your focus and press your way to completing the assignment?

3- Please share a few positive outcomes that you noted after completing one of your Kingdom assignments.

Affirmation: *I am Focused*

It can be said that having focus is important. However having the appropriate focus is critical. When your focus is blurred (cloudy) you cannot see clearly. Not seeing clearly can cause you to trip over things, miss the details, or even wind up headed in the wrong direction. "Focus" is a state or condition permitting clear percep- tion or understanding. Without focus, life will seem chaotic, con- fusing, and complicated. Have you ever looked through a camera and the focus was off? You could see objects but they were not clearly defined? As a result, you probably were a bit frustrated at trying to figure out the detail of what you were looking at. Just as with the lens on the camera that has limited focus, life without the proper focus can become very frustrating. You must be fo- cused on God and His plan for your life! When you are focused on God and His plan for your life you will have great perception and you will see "all" things clearly. Think back to the story of Peter walking on the water. As long as he was focused on God, he was able to walk on water, but when he became distracted and his focus shifted he almost drowned. Can you identify with this example? How many times have you been journeying through life with your focus on God and things were going well. Your household was peaceful, your job was profitable, and your rela- tionships were productive; but somehow your focus shifted from God to people or things and you began to drown in life's chaos?

You must get focused. Set your life in order with God as the head and let Him guide you in your endeavors. You must be focused!

Prayer: Thank You Lord, for the ability to focus on You and the Kingdom. I ask that You continually help me see clearly and precisely the plans You have for me. Help me to remain focused on Your Word and Your will for my life. Help me to develop tunnel vision when walking the path of life so that I will not become distracted by the things that are not of You. God as I begin to reflect over this affirmation and complete the reflective exercises, allow the Holy Spirit to remove any hindrances or distractions from my thoughts. In Jesus Name, Amen.

Reflective Exercise

1- What/who are you focused on?

2- Identify those things/people that have distracted you from pursuing more of God and the Kingdom?

3- What steps will you take to ensure you remain focused on God?

4- Describe your life when your focus was not clear? How has your life changed since your focus in clear?

Affirmation: *I am Fashioned*

You have been fashioned (shaped/formed) by God. He made you by hand and through His training God is molding you for greatness. Everything about you was formed by God, your eyes; your hair, your feet, and even your smile have been shaped by the Master artist Himself. God has fashioned you so that He can mold you into something great. You are in training so that you can reign in every area of your life! God has shaped and formed you for your particular purpose. You must understand that your fashion is perfect in Christ. You have been fashioned to be an heir in the Kingdom of God! You have been fashioned to be an over comer; overcoming those things that the world releases to kill you. You have been fashioned to be like Christ. In fact you have been created in His image and His likeness. You have been fashioned to sit in Heavenly places with Christ. You have been fashioned for God's glory.

Prayer: God, I thank You that I am fashioned. I thank You for planning every detail of my unique design. God, continue to mold me into what You desire for me to become. Help me to see the divine beauty within. God, as I begin to reflect over this affirma- tion and complete the reflective exercises, allow the Holy Spirit to remove any hindrances or distractions from my thoughts. In Jesus Name, Amen.

Reflective Exercise:

1- Describe your molding process. What has been the most difficult and most exciting part of the process thus far?

2- While enduring the molding process; was it difficult for you to become pliable (bendable) for God, why or why not?

3- Can you think of a time when God was trying to bend you and you were not allowing Him to perform His perfect work? What was the outcome?

Affirmation: *I am Faithful*

Are you faithful? What or who are you faithful to? Do you adhere to the directives of God? Being faithful to God allows you the opportunity to advance in the Kingdom. God's Word tells us in Deuteronomy 11:13, "if you faithfully obey the commands I am giving you today—to love the LORD your God and to serve Him with all your heart and with all your soul- 14 then I will send rain on your land in its season, both autumn and spring rains, so that you may gather in your grain, new wine and oil. 15 I will provide grass in the fields for your cattle, and you will eat and be satis- fied". All you have to do is be faithful to God and He will bless you. Be full of faith. Trust God even when it is difficult, trust God even when you do not feel like it. The word "faith" is defined in Hebrews 11 as the substance of things hoped for and the evidence of things not seen. So when you do not see the blessing coming, be faithful to God anyway, when you do not receive the position you so desire, be faithful to God, be faithful over the few things (your household, your job, your loved ones) and God will make you ruler over many! Build your faith (full of God) today!

Prayer: Dear Lord, please help me to become more faithful? Help me to walk by faith and not by sight. Guide me every step of the way in this walk of faith. Help me to realize that You are in control every step of the way. God, as I begin to reflect over this affirmation and complete the reflective exercises, allow the Holy Spirit to remove any hindrances or distractions from my thoughts. In Jesus Name, Amen!

Reflective Exercise:

1- Who/what are you faithful to?

2- How can you improve in your faith walk with Christ?

3- How will you begin to be more faithful in the things God has given to you? Finances, Health, Family, Job, etc.

Affirmation: *I* am Dedicated

Many times we find ourselves being dedicated to our family, career, and social entities. But the most important question is are you dedicated to God? When you are dedicated, you are devoted to a cause or purpose. Many of us are dedicated to social organizations, political stances, or particular groups; but, when it comes to God that dedication seems to take a back seat. In the Kingdom, do you spend time focusing on a particular cause, such as evangelism, Kingdom administration, or Kingdom education? Do you set aside time specifically for the Kingdom? When you are devoted to something you take great joy in participating in it even if you do not see a great return. The good news about Kingdom devotion/participation is that there is a guaranteed result of eternal life with our Heavenly Father. When you are dedicated to the Kingdom no one has to beg you to give assistance in your church body? No one has to ask you to sow seed into the finances of the church body. You just do it, because you are devoted (dedicated). God is dedicated to each of us and He shows His dedication in various ways: the constant extension of His grace and mercy, His forgiveness, His compassion, and His love. Are you dedicated to God and His cause to build His Kingdom? Give back to God as He has given much to you.

Prayer: God it is my desire that I become dedicated to Your Kingdom. I want to be focused on Your work and I want to dedicate all that I have and all that I am for Your total/complete use. God help me to devote my time, talent, and resources to Your people. God, as I begin to reflect over this affirmation and com- plete the reflective exercises, allow the Holy Spirit to remove any hindrances or distractions from my thoughts, In Jesus Name, Amen!

Reflective Exercise

1-Think of at least one situation where an obstacle you faced lowered your level of determination; what steps did you take to surpass those obstacles.

2- What steps can you take to become dedicated in the area(s) listed in question 1?

3- Write out your personal declaration to the Kingdom of God.

Affirmation: *I* am Determined

Have you ever been determined to do something? Nothing or no one could stop you once you became determined. All you could think about was what would happen when you accomplished that one thing that you were determined to accomplish. It began with a mental picture, it formed an inner thought, you devised a plan to achieve it, and you became determined to see it come to pass. Just like it was with that one thing you so desired to have and were determined to obtain; are you determined to live a life that is Holy and pleasing to our God? Are you determined to put the will of God for your life ahead of all that you do? Determination is a powerful force. It is determination that makes you get up every morning (you are determined to experience life), it is determination that pushes you to go to work (you are determined to have your needs met), it is determination that makes you pursue an education (you are determined to become the best you can in the career field you choose). However, it is the determination to live a life in Christ that is most important. Be determined to walk upright before God. Determination will give you wings to soar above defeat. Indeed it will give you the fortitude to surpass your obstacles. Ultimately, it will give you the ability to see the victory while you are going through the battle. Be determined today, be more like Christ, walk upright before Him, live a life that is pleasing to Him, and lead the lost to Him.

Prayer: God, help me with my level of determination. I want to have a mind that is fixed on You and Your Kingdom. God, please help me to increase my level of determination for You and Your people. God as I begin to reflect over this affirmation and complete the reflective exercises, allow the Holy Spirit to re- move any hindrances or distractions from my thoughts. In Jesus Name, Amen.

Reflective Exercise

1- Write a list of what you are determined to do in/for the Kingdom?

2- Have you begun working on those things listed in question 1? If so, how will you continue to walk those things out? If not how will you fuel your determination to complete the list?

3- Think of at least one situation where an obstacle you faced lowered your level of determination. What steps did you take to surpass those obstacles?

Affirmation: *I am Destined*

Do you realize that you are destined for greatness! It has been decreed (determined/commanded) that you will be great and will achieve great things. In Jeremiah 1, the Lord says, "before I formed you in the womb, I knew you; before you were born, I set you apart and consecrated you". God did this for Jeremiah, because He knew Jeremiah was destined, He had a destination for Jeremiah and He has a destination for you. In Jeremiah 29:11, the word says, "for I know the plans I have for you, plans to prosper you and not harm you to give you hope and a future". God has destined you for a purpose of greatness.! Please know and understand that where you are right now is not the end; and where you are going is greater than any place you have ever been. Your destination in Christ allows you to be seated in Heavenly places far above the troubles of the world. You must understand that you are destined by God to be who He says you are, do what He says you can do, and have all that He says you can have. Enjoy the ride, because you are destined for greatness in Christ!

Prayer: Lord, help me to understand that I am destined for greatness in You and my destination is beyond the place I am presently in. Help me to stay focused on Your word and to use Your Word as a road map to my final destination (in Heaven, with You and my Father). God as I begin to reflect over this affirmation and complete the reflective exercises, allow the Holy Spirit to remove any hindrances or distractions from my thoughts. In Jesus Name, Amen.

Reflective Exercise

1- What are at least two things you feel God has destined you to do with/in your life?

2- What steps are you taking to complete those two things?

3- What are the hindrances you have faced in completing those two things?

4- How do you plan to surpass those hindrances?

Affirmation: *I am Fearfully and Wonderfully made*

One of my favorite scriptures in the Bible is Psalm 139. This scripture talks about how God knows us on an intimate level and that He is with us in all situations. Verse 14 says that I am fearfully and wonderfully made! My dear sisters; you are fearfully (full of awe or reverence) and wonderfully (unusually good; admirable) made. You have been put together piece by piece with a destination rooted in greatness. I know that you have heard the cliché, "God does not make any junk, believe it because it is true, God does not make any junk"; God only creates the best and has the best intention for each of us. His Word says in the book of Jeremiah, "for I know the plans I have for you declares the Lord, plans to prosper and not to harm you, to give you hope and an expected end". God made you from some dynamic and ecstatic DNA, so that you could prosper for the Kingdom. God developed your blue print and then fashioned you to fit it. Never think that you are not made of good stuff. Always remember that you are made exceptionally well by the Master Potter Himself. I decree and declare today, my sister that you are fearfully and wonderfully made.

Victorious Affirmations For Women

Prayer: Dear Lord please help me to recognize that I am fearfully and wonderfully made! I pray that I will see myself through Your eyes and understand that my DNA is unique. Please help me to remove those traits and behaviors that are not like You. God as I begin to reflect over this affirmation and complete the reflective exercises, allow the Holy Spirit to remove any hindrances or distractions from my thoughts. In Jesus Name, Amen.

Reflective Exercise

1- Write down at least three traits/behaviors that you have and are uncomfortable with. After reading Psalm 139, are you willing to allow God to search you and change those traits/behaviors.

2- Ask God to illuminate those traits and behaviors that are not like Him. Write an action step for each behavior/train you need to change

3- For ever behavior/trait that you need to change, write a positive affirmation that you will declare over the next 10 days. At the end of the 10 days write down how this exercise has changed your perspective.

Affirmation: *I* am Victorious

Do you realize that you are a victor and it is ordained that you be victorious in all that you do? The word of God states, that the Lord your God is the one who goes with you to fight for you against your enemies to give you victory. You must realize, that with this being a fact (because God's word cannot lie), then you automatically have victory. One thing that I have learned from this passage of scripture is that if God is the one that goes before you to fight against your enemies to give you victory, then your battle is a sanctified set up, you cannot loose and thus you are victorious. Whichever (situation you are facing) know that you have the victory! God knows all about the adversary (bills, addiction, or the job) and He can devise a plan for you to win over them. Simply put; every battle that comes your way God has already set you up for victory. God not only knows about the adversary but He tells you how you must fight the battle (ensuring that you are victorious). The final thing that He does is, He lets you know how you must fight. His Word tells us the weapons we fight with (2 Corinthians 10:4-5), then He tells us the things that we fight against (Ephesians 6:12), and then He tells us how we should dress for the battle (Ephesians 6:14-17), so with all of this knowl- edge you cannot lose any battle and you must be victorious.

Victorious Affirmations For Women

Prayer: God I thank You for my victory over all circumstances and situations. I am grateful that I will develop a constant thought pattern as a victor and not a victim. I thank You God for helping me to see each battle that I face as an opportunity for you to use me for Your Glory and to defeat satan and his army. God as I begin to reflect over this affirmation and complete the reflec- tive exercises, allow the Holy Spirit to remove any hindrances or distractions from my thoughts. In Jesus Name, Amen.

Reflective Exercise

1- Share a time when you battled a situation and felt that you lost. After reading this affirmation can you share your new perspective.

2- What is one of the most difficult battles you have faced? Can you say that you prepared yourself to do battle by recognizing that God has told you how to fight, what you were fighting against, and what protective armor to wear? If not, what will you do different when the next battle presents itself?

Affirmation: *I am* Celebrated

Don't you just love celebrations? It feels good when you take part in a celebration, sharing in someone's achievements and their blessings! Today I want to celebrate you for being an awesome woman of God! I want you to know that you are very special to me and I appreciate your love for supporting this project and for sowing into my gifting for the Kingdom. I celebrate you because you are:

Child of God: John 1:2, 1John 3:1

Over comer: 1 John 5:4-5 You can overcome "all" things that come your way

New Creation: 2 Corinthians 5:17

Minister of Reconciliation: 2 Corinthians 5:18-19

Christ Ambassador: 2 Corinthians 5:20

Victorious Affirmations For Women

Redeemed: 1 Corinthians 6:19-20

Seated with Christ in Heavenly Realms: Ephesians 2:6-7

Priest: 1 Peter 2:5

Foreknown, Predestined, Called, Justified, and Glorified: Romans 8:29-30

Heir of God and Co-heir with Christ: Romans 8:17

Reflective Exercise:

Please share your thoughts with me. I would like you to answer the following questions:

What was the most inspiring/encouraging affirmation that you read?

Please share a brief testimony of how this book helped you?

Please send e-mails to: victoriousaffirmations@yahoo.com

www.ingramcontent.com/pod-product-compliance
Lightning Source LLC
Chambersburg PA
CBHW032217040426
42449CB00005B/649